D0537410

by Iain Gray

Lang**Syne**

PUBLISHING

WRITING *to* REMEMBER

Lang**Syne**

PUBLISHING

WRITING *to* REMEMBER

Vineyard Business Centre,
Pathhead, Midlothian EH37 5XP
Tel: 01875 321 203 Fax: 01875 321 233
E-mail: info@lang-syne.co.uk
www.langsyneshop.co.uk

Design by Dorothy Meikle
Printed by Montgomery Litho, Glasgow
© Lang Syne Publishers Ltd 2011

ISBN 978-1-85217-252-7

Dunne

MOTTO:
The people of the hill forever
(or) Victory from the hills
(or) The summit to victory.

CREST:
A lizard in front of a holly bush.

NAME variations include:
Ó Duinn *(Gaelic)*
Donn
Dun
Dunn
O' Doinn
O' Dunn
O' Dunne
O' Doyne

Ireland's loss, however, was to the gain of the countries in which the immigrants settled, contributing enormously, as their descendants do today, to the well being of the nations in which their forefathers settled.

But those who were forced through dire circumstance to establish a new life in foreign parts never forgot their roots, or the proud heritage and traditions of the land that gave them birth.

Nor do their descendants.

It is a heritage that is inextricably bound up in the colourful variety of Irish names themselves – and the origin and history of these names forms an integral part of the vibrant drama that is the nation's history, one of both glorious fortune and tragic misfortune.

This history is well documented, and one of the most important and fascinating of the earliest sources are *The Annals of the Four Masters*, compiled between 1632 and 1636 by four friars at the Franciscan Monastery in County Donegal.

Compiled from earlier sources, and purporting to go back to the Biblical Deluge, much of the material takes in the mythological origins and history of Ireland and the Irish.

This includes tales of successive waves of invaders and settlers such as the Fomorians, the Partholonians, the Nemedians, the Fir Bolgs, the Tuatha De Danann, and the Laigain.

Of particular interest are the *Milesian Genealogies*,

because the majority of Irish clans today claim a descent from either Heremon, Ir, or Heber – three of the sons of Milesius, a king of what is now modern day Spain.

These sons invaded Ireland in the second millennium B.C, apparently in fulfilment of a mysterious prophecy received by their father.

This Milesian lineage is said to have ruled Ireland for nearly 3,000 years, until the island came under the sway of England's King Henry II in 1171 following what is known as the Cambro-Norman invasion.

This is an important date not only in Irish history in general, but for the effect the invasion subsequently had for Irish surnames.

'Cambro' comes from the Welsh, and 'Cambro-Norman' describes those Welsh knights of Norman origin who invaded Ireland.

But they were invaders who stayed, inter-marrying with the native Irish population and founding their own proud dynasties that bore Cambro-Norman names such as Archer, Barbour, Brannagh, Fitzgerald, Fitzgibbon, Fleming, Joyce, Plunkett, and Walsh – to name only a few.

These 'Cambro-Norman' surnames that still flourish throughout the world today form one of the three main categories in which Irish names can be placed – those of Gaelic-Irish, Cambro-Norman, and Anglo-Irish.

Previous to the Cambro-Norman invasion of the twelfth century, and throughout the earlier invasions and settlement of those wild bands of sea rovers known as the Vikings in the eighth and ninth centuries, the population of the island was relatively small, and it was normal for a person to be identified through the use of only a forename.

But as population gradually increased and there were many more people with the same forename, surnames were adopted to distinguish one person, or one community, from another.

Individuals identified themselves with their own particular tribe, or 'tuath', and this tribe – that also became known as a clann, or clan – took its name from some distinguished ancestor who had founded the clan.

The Gaelic-Irish form of the name Kelly, for example, is Ó Ceallaigh, or O'Kelly, indicating descent from an original 'Ceallaigh', with the 'O' denoting 'grandson of.' The name was later anglicised to Kelly.

The prefix 'Mac' or 'Mc', meanwhile, as with the clans of the Scottish Highlands, denotes 'son of.'

Although the Irish clans had much in common with their Scottish counterparts, one important difference lies in what are known as 'septs', or branches, of the clan.

Septs of Scottish clans were groups who often bore an entirely different name from the clan name but were under the clan's protection.

In Ireland, septs were groups that shared the same name and who could be found scattered throughout the four provinces of Ulster, Leinster, Munster, and Connacht.

The 'golden age' of the Gaelic-Irish clans, infused as their veins were with the blood of Celts, pre-dates the Viking invasions of the eighth and ninth centuries and the Norman invasion of the twelfth century, and the sacred heart of the country was the Hill of Tara, near the River Boyne, in County Meath.

Known in Gaelic as 'Teamhar na Rí', or Hill of Kings, it was the royal seat of the 'Ard Rí Éireann', or High King of Ireland, to whom the petty kings, or chieftains, from the island's provinces were ultimately subordinate.

It was on the Hill of Tara, beside a stone pillar known as the Irish 'Lia Fáil', or Stone of Destiny, that the High Kings were inaugurated and, according to legend, this stone would emit a piercing screech that could be heard all over Ireland when touched by the hand of the rightful king.

The Hill of Tara is today one of the island's main tourist attractions.

Opposition to English rule over Ireland, established in the wake of the Cambro-Norman invasion, broke out frequently and the harsh solution adopted by the powerful forces of the Crown was to forcibly evict the native Irish from their lands.

These lands were then granted to Protestant colonists, or 'planters', from Britain.

Many of these colonists, ironically, came from Scotland and were the descendants of the original 'Scotti', or 'Scots', who gave their name to Scotland after migrating there in the fifth century A.D., from the north of Ireland.

Colonisation entailed harsh penal laws being imposed on the majority of the native Irish population, stripping them practically of all of their rights.

The Crown's main bastion in Ireland was Dublin and its environs, known as the Pale, and it was the dispossessed peasantry who lived outside this Pale, desperately striving to eke out a meagre living.

It was this that gave rise to the modern-day expression of someone or something being 'beyond the pale'.

Attempts were made to stamp out all aspects of the ancient Gaelic-Irish culture, to the extent that even to bear a Gaelic-Irish name was to invite discrimination.

This is why many Gaelic-Irish names were anglicised with, for example, and noted above, Ó Ceallaigh, or O'Kelly, being anglicised to Kelly.

Succeeding centuries have seen strong revivals of Gaelic-Irish consciousness, however, and this has led to many families reverting back to the original form of their name, while the language itself is frequently found on the fluent tongues of an estimated 90,000 to 145,000 of the island's population.

Ireland's turbulent history of religious and political strife is one that lasted well into the twentieth century, a landmark century that saw the partition of the island into the twenty-six counties of the independent Republic of

Ireland, or Eire, and the six counties of Northern Ireland, or Ulster.

Dublin, originally founded by Vikings, is now a vibrant and truly cosmopolitan city while the proud city of Belfast is one of the jewels in the crown of Ulster.

It was Saint Patrick who first brought the light of Christianity to Ireland in the fifth century A.D.

Interpretations of this Christian message have varied over the centuries, often leading to bitter sectarian conflict – but the many intricately sculpted Celtic Crosses found all over the island are symbolic of a unity that crosses the sectarian divide.

It is an image that fuses the 'old gods' of the Celts with Christianity.

All the signs from the early years of this new millennium indicate that sectarian strife may soon become a thing of the past – with the Irish and their many kinsfolk across the world, be they Protestant or Catholic, finding common purpose in the rich tapestry of their shared heritage.

Chapter two:
High Kings

In its Gaelic form of Ó Duinn, the name of Dunne is commonly thought to stem from a word indicating 'brown', as in 'brown-haired', although another interesting theory is that it stems from 'dun', meaning a hill.

This, some sources assert, explains the Dunne motto of 'Mullach Abú', variously thought to mean 'The people of the hill forever', 'Victory from the hills' or 'The summit to victory.'

Whatever the origins of the name, the Dunnes flourished for centuries mainly in the present day counties of Kildare and Laois (also known as Queen's County).

It was through a branch of the great O' Connor Clan known as Uí Failghe that some of the Dunne septs traced a descent from a legendary Irish High King who was a contemporary and a rival of yet another legendary warrior king.

The High King from whom the Dunnes trace a descent was Catháir Mór, who is thought to have reigned as Ard Rí, or High King, from between 119 and 122 A.D.

His reign ended in dramatic and bloody fashion at the hands of the gloriously named Conn Céthchathach, the Gaelic form for Conn of the Hundred Battles.

One of Conn's illustrious ancestors is said to have been

no less than Goidel Glas, who is reputed to have created the Gaelic-Irish language after he combined and refined the 72 known languages of his time.

As a youth, Conn is said to have met two mysterious figures who predicted he and his descendants would rule Ireland.

The strange figures who are reputed by legend to have appeared to Conn, enshrouded in mist, were a beautiful young maiden known as Sovranty.

Wearing a golden crown and seated on a crystal chair, she was accompanied by the sun god Lugh, patron of arts and crafts.

It is said they prophesied his descendants would rule until the death of the old Gods – which in fact did occur in the form of St. Patrick and the new religion of Christianity.

Conn attained the High Kingship after killing Catháir Mór at the battle of Moigh Acha, in present day Co. Meath.

But his kingship was never secure because he had to fight a relentless succession of battles with his great rival Eogan Mór, also known as Mug Nadhat, king of the Dál nAraide, or Cruithe, who occupied the northeastern territories of Ireland.

It was because of the number of battles Conn fought with these Cruithne, or Picts, that he earned the title of Conn Céthchathach – Conn of the Hundred Battles.

The two rival kings achieved a temporary accommodation after the island was divided between themselves, the division starting at a ridge known as Eiscir Riada, which traverses the island from Galway Bay to Dublin.

Mug's territory in the south was known as Leth Moga Nuadht, while Conn's northern territory was known as Leth Cuinn.

But it was not long before the ambitious and fiercely proud pair were at each other's throats again.

Mug gained the upper hand for a time after storing up grain in his territories after taking heed of a dire Druidic prophecy of famine – but Conn eventually defeated his rival after taking him by cunning surprise in a night raid near present-day Tullamore, in County Offaly.

Conn consolidated his kingship over Ireland, but his success was short-lived, destined to die under the glinting blades of fifty warriors who had managed to breach the defences of his royal bastion of Tara after disguising themselves as women.

At the head of these warriors was the vengeful Tibride Tirech, son of Catháir Mór, whom Conn had killed several years earlier.

In later centuries the Dunne descendants of Catháir Mór reigned supreme from a fortress in the area of present day Tinnahinch, in Co. Laois.

Later known as Tinnahinch Castle, this was a stronghold that would serve them well until its destruction in the mid-seventeenth century at the hands of vengeful invaders.

The door to these seventeenth century invaders had first been wrenched open in the late twelfth century by Norman invaders.

Twelfth century Ireland was far from being a unified nation, split up as it was into territories ruled over by squabbling chieftains who ruled as kings in their own right – and this inter-clan rivalry worked to the advantage of the invaders.

In a series of bloody conflicts one chieftain, or king, would occasionally gain the upper hand over his rivals, and by 1156 the most powerful was Muirchertach MacLochlainn, king of the powerful O' Neills.

The equally powerful Rory O' Connor, king of the province of Connacht, opposed him but he increased his power and influence by allying himself with Dermot MacMurrough, king of Leinster.

MacLochlainn and MacMurrough were aware that the main key to the kingdom of Ireland was the thriving trading port of Dublin that had been established by invading Vikings, or Ostmen, in 852 A.D.

Dublin was taken by the combined forces of the Leinster and Connacht kings, but when MacLochlainn died the Dubliners rose up in revolt and overthrew the unpopular MacMurrough.

A triumphant Rory O'Connor entered Dublin and was later inaugurated as Ard Rí, but MacMurrough refused to accept defeat.

He appealed for help from England's Henry II in unseating O'Connor, an act that was to radically affect the future course of Ireland's fortunes.

The English monarch agreed to help MacMurrough, but distanced himself from direct action by delegating his Norman subjects in Wales with the task.

These ambitious and battle-hardened barons and knights had first settled in Wales following the Norman Conquest of England in 1066 and, with an eye on rich booty, plunder, and lands, were only too eager to obey their sovereign's wishes and furnish MacMurrough with aid.

MacMurrough rallied powerful barons such as Robert Fitzstephen and Maurice Fitzgerald to his cause, along with Gilbert de Clare, Earl of Pembroke.

The mighty Norman war machine soon exploded into action, and so fierce and disciplined was their onslaught on the forces of Rory O'Connor and his allies that by 1171 they had re-captured Dublin and other strategically important territories.

Henry II began to take cold feet over the venture, realising that he may have created a rival in the form of a separate Norman kingdom in Ireland.

Accordingly, he landed on the island, near Waterford, at the head of a large army in October of 1171 with the aim of curbing the power of his Cambro-Norman barons.

But protracted war between the king and his barons was averted when they submitted to the royal will, promising homage and allegiance in return for holding the territories they had conquered in the king's name.

Henry also received the reluctant submission and homage of many of the Irish chieftains, and English dominion over Ireland was ratified through the Treaty of Windsor of 1175.

Under its terms Rory O'Connor, for example, was allowed to rule territory unoccupied by the Normans in the role of a vassal of the king.

It was a recipe for rebellion as some Dunnes, for example, were driven from their ancient homelands in favour of the Norman Fitzgeralds.

Chapter three:

Oppression and rebellion

As the English grip on Ireland tightened, the island groaned under a weight of oppression that was directed in the main against native Irish clans such as the Dunnes.

An indication of the harsh treatment meted out to them can be found in a desperate plea sent to Pope John XII by Roderick O'Carroll of Ely, Donald O'Neill of Ulster, and a number of other Irish chieftains in 1318.

They stated: 'As it very constantly happens, whenever an Englishman, by perfidy or craft, kills an Irishman, however noble, or however innocent, be he clergy or layman, there is no penalty or correction enforced against the person who may be guilty of such wicked murder.

'But rather the more eminent the person killed and the higher rank which he holds among his own people, so much more is the murderer honoured and rewarded by the English, and not merely by the people at large, but also by the religious and bishops of the English race.'

But resistance did not only take the form of written appeals, with many native Irish such as the Dunnes literally taking to the hills and engaging in bitter guerrilla warfare with the forces of the Crown.

One base of the Dunnes was the Slieve Bloom

mountains, from where they would launch lightning raids on English garrisons and townships.

But ultimate victory was to be denied them as the English Crown extended its despised policy of 'plantation', or settlement of loyal Protestants on land held by native Irish such as the Dunnes

The policy had started during the reign from 1491 to 1547 of Henry VIII, whose Reformation effectively outlawed the established Roman Catholic faith throughout his dominions.

It continued throughout the subsequent reigns of Elizabeth I, James I (James VI of Scotland), and in the wake of the Cromwellian invasion of 1649.

In an insurrection that exploded in 1641, at least 2,000 Protestant settlers were massacred at the hands of Catholic landowners and their native Irish peasantry, while thousands more were driven from their lands to seek refuge where they could.

Dunnes were at the forefront of this rebellion, with a David Dunne and his kinsmen successfully laying siege to and later destroying the stronghold belonging to Sir Charles Coote known as Castlecuffe.

It was an act for which the Dunnes would later pay dearly.

Terrible as the atrocities were against the Protestant settlers, subsequent accounts became greatly exaggerated, serving to fuel a burning desire on the part of Protestants for revenge against the rebels.

The English Civil War intervened to prevent immediate

action against the rebels, but following the execution of Charles I in 1649 and the consolidation of the power of England's fanatically Protestant Oliver Cromwell, the time was ripe for revenge.

The Lord Protector, as he was named, descended on Ireland at the head of a 20,000-strong army that landed at Ringford, near Dublin, in August of 1649, and the consequences of this Cromwellian conquest still resonate throughout the island today.

Cromwell had three main aims: to quash all forms of rebellion, to 'remove' all Catholic landowners who had taken part in the rebellion, and to convert the native Irish to the Protestant faith.

An early warning of the terrors that were in store for the native Catholic Irish came when the northeastern town of Drogheda was stormed and taken in September and between 2,000 and 4,000 of its inhabitants killed, including priests who were summarily put to the sword.

Cromwell soon held the island in a grip of iron, allowing him to implement what amounted to a policy of ethnic cleansing.

His troopers were given free rein to hunt down and kill priests, while Catholic estates, such as those of the Dunnes, were confiscated. The Dunne stronghold of Tinnahinch finally fell to Cromwellian troopers in 1653 and was destroyed.

An estimated 11 million acres of land were confiscated and the dispossessed native Irish banished to Connacht and Co. Clare.

An edict was issued stating that any native Irish found east of the River Shannon after May 1, 1654 faced either summary execution or transportation to the West Indies.

The final death knell of the ancient Gaelic order of proud families such as the Dunnes came in the form of what is known in Ireland as Cogadh an Dá Rí, or The War of the Two Kings.

Also known as the Williamite War in Ireland or the Jacobite War in Ireland, it was sparked off in 1688 when the Stuart monarch James II (James VII of Scotland) was deposed and fled into exile in France.

The Protestant William of Orange and his wife Mary were invited to take up the thrones of Scotland, Ireland, and England – but James still had significant support in Ireland.

His supporters were known as Jacobites, and among them were several Dunnes.

Following the arrival in England of William and Mary from Holland, Richard Talbot, 1st Earl of Tyrconnell and James's Lord Deputy in Ireland, assembled an army loyal to the Stuart cause.

The aim was to garrison and fortify the island in the name of James and quell any resistance.

Londonderry, or Derry, proved loyal to the cause of William of Orange, or William III as he had become, and managed to hold out against a siege that was not lifted until July 28, 1689.

James, with the support of troops and money supplied by Louis XIV of France, had landed at Kinsale in March of 1689 and joined forces with his Irish supporters.

A series of military encounters followed, culminating in James's defeat by an army commanded by William at the battle of the Boyne on July 12, 1689.

James fled again into French exile, never to return, while another significant Jacobite defeat occurred in July of 1691 at the battle of Aughrim – with about half their army killed on the field, wounded, or taken prisoner.

Among the dead were a Lieutenant Colonel Dunne and a Captain Terence Dunne.

The Williamite forces besieged Limerick and the Jacobites were forced into surrender in September of 1691.

A peace treaty, known as the Treaty of Limerick followed, under which those Jacobites willing to swear an oath of loyalty to William were allowed to remain in their native land.

Those reluctant to do so, including many Dunnes, were allowed to seek exile on foreign shores – but their ancient homelands were lost to them forever.

A further flight overseas occurred following an abortive rebellion in 1798, while Dunnes were among the many thousands of Irish who were forced to seek a new life many thousands of miles from their native land during the famine known as The Great Hunger, caused by a failure of the potato crop between 1845 and 1849.

But in many cases Ireland's loss of sons and daughters such as the Dunnes was to the gain of those equally proud nations in which they settled.

Chapter four:

On the world stage

Bearers of the proud name of Dunne, in all the variety of spellings of the name, have achieved celebrity through a wide range of pursuits.

One family of Dunnes in particular are notable on the American literary and acting scene.

Born in 1925 in Hartford, Connecticut, **Dominick Dunne** is the investigative journalist, writer, and former Hollywood producer who has covered a number of famous trials for American Court TV, including that of O.J. Simpson.

His concern over justice and injustice stemmed from the murder of his actress daughter, **Dominique Dunne**, in 1982.

Born in 1959 in Santa Monica, Dominique Dunne's most famous role was as the eldest daughter, Dana, in the movie *Poltergeist*, although she had also appeared in a number of television series such as *Hart to Hart* and *Fame*.

It was shortly after completing work on *Poltergeist* that she was murdered at the hands of a former lover.

Her father attended her killer's trial and later wrote *Justice: A Father's Account of the Trial of his Daughter's Killer* while her mother, Ellen, founded the victims' rights organisation Justice for Homicide Victims.

Born in 1955 in New York City and a brother of Dominique Dunne, **Griffin Dunne** is the American actor and film director whose film roles include the 1981 *American Werewolf in London*, the 1985 *After Hours*, the 1987 *Johnny Dangerously* and the 1991 *My Girl*.

He has also appeared in a number of popular television series including *Frasier*, *Alias*, and *Law and Order*.

His uncle, **John Gregory Dunne**, was the novelist, literary critic, and screenwriter who was born in Hartford, Connecticut in 1923 and died in 2003.

Married to the novelist Joan Didion, he collaborated with her on a number of screenplays that included the 1971 *Panic in Needle Park* and *A Star is Born*, from 1976.

Their screenplay for the 1981 *True Confessions* was adapted from his own novel, while he was also the author of the non-fiction books concerning the Hollywood film industry, *Monster* and *The Studio*.

Mary Chavelita Dunn, born in 1859 in Australia, was the writer and feminist also known Mary Chavelita Dunne Bright, but better known by her pen name of George Egerton.

It was under this name that the writer and fighter for women's rights wrote books such as *Now Spring Has Come*, first published in 1890. She died in 1945.

Also in the literary world **Finley Peter Dunne**, born in 1867 in Chicago and who died in 1936, was the writer and humorist responsible for the famed *Mr Dooley* articles that first appeared in a Chicago newspaper and were later syndicated throughout the country.

'Mr Dooley' was a fictional Irish-American bartender who would dispense his wit and wisdom to the patrons of his Chicago bar – and among his many fans was no less than President Theodore Roosevelt.

Dunne later moved to New York, where he edited a number of celebrated magazines that included *Metropolitan Magazine* and *Collier's Weekly*.

Famous quotes from Dunne's witty pen include 'Trust everybody, but cut the cards', 'Alcohol is necessary for a man so that now and then he can have a good opinion of himself, undisturbed by the facts', and 'Minds are like parachutes. They only function when they are open.'

His son was the Hollywood film director, producer and screenwriter **Philip Dunne**, who was born in New York City in 1908 and who died in 1992.

His many screen credits include he 1941 *How Green Was My Valley*, the 1953 *The Robe*, and the 1965 *The Agony and the Ecstasy*.

Dunne, who has a star on the Hollywood Walk of Fame, was also a co-founder in 1947 of an organisation set up to protest against the House Un-American Activities Committee's investigation into alleged Communist influence in Hollywood.

On the stage **Irene Dunne** was the five-time Academy

Award-nominated actress who was born Irene Marie Dunn in 1898 in Louisville, Kentucky.

Her Broadway debut came in 1922 in a stage production of Arthur Miller's *The Clinging Voice*, but it was her role as Magnolia Hawks in a production of Kern and Hammerstein's *Show Boat* that first brought her to the attention of Hollywood.

She reprised the role in the 1936 screen version of the musical and went on to star in a number of other movies.

Described as 'the best actress to never win an Academy Award', she was the recipient of five nominations for Best Actress – for the 1931 *Cimarron*, the 1936 *Theodora Goes Wild, The Awful Truth*, from 1937, the 1939 *Love Affair* and the 1948 *I Remember Mama*.

She retired from the stage in 1952 and was appointed five years later by President Dwight D. Eisenhower as a delegate to the United Nations, in recognition of her work with both the Republican Party and a number of charitable causes.

She and her husband, the New York dentist Francis Griffin, were also ordained Knights of Malta in recognition of their work for Roman Catholic charities.

The actress, who died in 1990, has a star on the Hollywood Walk of Fame.

Also on the stage **Robin Dunne**, born in 1976 in Toronto, is the Canadian actor known for his film roles in *As*

If and *Species 3* in addition to television roles in *Dead Like Me* and *Dawson's Creek*.

In the highly competitive world of sport **Ben Dunne** is the Irish professional boxer who was born in Neilston, Dublin in 1980.

Since his first professional fight in 2001 the super bantamweight boxer has, at the time of writing, has lost only one of his 25 fights; nicknamed 'the Dublin Dynamo', he took the European Super Bantamweight title in November of 2006, but lost it in August of 2007.

The Republic of Ireland has also produced some talented European footballers.

Born in Dublin in 1941 **Tony Dunne** is the former left back who was awarded 33 caps with the Republic of Ireland team between 1962 and 1975. Teams he played for included Shelbourne, Manchester United, the American Detroit Express, and Bolton Wanderers, while he has also managed teams that include Bolton Wanderers.

Nicknamed 'Dunney Monster', **Richard Dunne** is the 6ft. 2in. tall football defender who was born in Dublin in 1979. A player with the national team he plays, at the time of writing, for Manchester City.

Still on the football pitch **Jimmy Dunne**, born in Ringsend, Co. Dublin in 1905 and who died in 1949, was the forward who was the first Irishman to play a major role in the English League – playing for teams that included Sheffield United, Arsenal, and Southampton.

In the world of the judiciary, **Charles Dunn**, born in 1799 in Bullet County, Kentucky to an Irish father and an American mother, was the lawyer who rose to become Chief Justice of the Territory of Wisconsin.

Born in 1853 in Watertown, Connecticut, **Edward Fitzsimmons Dunne** was the American Democrat politician who served as Mayor of Chicago from 1905 to 1907 and as Governor of Illinois from 1913 to 1917.

In the world of medicine **Sir Patrick Dun**, born in 1642 in Aberdeen, was the Scottish physician and later President of the Royal College of Physicians who founded a hospital in Dublin that bears his name to this day.

On the field of battle **Colonel Humphrey O' Dunne** was a noted soldier of the American Civil War, while **Captain Philip Dunne**, born in 1904 and who died in 1965, was the English soldier and later politician who was awarded the Military Cross in 1943 for his service with a special commando unit in the Middle East.

One Dunne who had a particularly fertile and inventive mind was the Irishman John William Dunne, better known as **J.W. Dunne**, who was born in 1875 in Co. Kildare.

His father General Sir John Hart Dunne was a distinguished soldier who had fought in the Crimean War of 1854, and his son followed in his father's footsteps when he enlisted in the ranks of the British Army during the Second Boer War of 1901.

It was while serving in the army that he became involved in what was then the fledgling field of military aviation.

By 1904 he had invented a special type of aerofoil and later built and flew a number of monoplanes and biplanes, including the first British military aeroplane.

Dunne was also fascinated with the concept of time and in two books, the 1927 *An Experiment With Time* and the 1934 *The Serial Universe*, put forward the intriguing theory that past, present, and future actually occur simultaneously.

He died in 1949.

Key dates in Ireland's history from the first settlers to the formation of the Irish Republic:

circa 7000 B.C. Arrival and settlement of Stone Age people.

circa 3000 B.C. Arrival of settlers of New Stone Age period.

circa 600 B.C. First arrival of the Celts.

200 A.D. Establishment of Hill of Tara, Co. Meath, as seat of the High Kings.

circa 432 A.D. Christian mission of St. Patrick.

800-920 A.D. Invasion and subsequent settlement of Vikings.

1002 A.D. Brian Boru recognised as High King.

1014 Brian Boru killed at battle of Clontarf.

1169-1170 Cambro-Norman invasion of the island.

1171 Henry II claims Ireland for the English Crown.

1366 Statutes of Kilkenny ban marriage between native Irish and English.

1529-1536 England's Henry VIII embarks on religious Reformation.

1536 Earl of Kildare rebels against the Crown.

1541 Henry VIII declared King of Ireland.

1558 Accession to English throne of Elizabeth I.

1565 Battle of Affane.

1569-1573 First Desmond Rebellion.

1579-1583 Second Desmond Rebellion.

1594-1603 Nine Years War.

1606 Plantation' of Scottish and English settlers.

1607	Flight of the Earls.
1632-1636	Annals of the Four Masters compiled.
1641	Rebellion over policy of plantation and other grievances.
1649	Beginning of Cromwellian conquest.
1688	Flight into exile in France of Catholic Stuart monarch James II as Protestant Prince William of Orange invited to take throne of England along with his wife, Mary.
1689	William and Mary enthroned as joint monarchs; siege of Derry.
1690	Jacobite forces of James defeated by William at battle of the Boyne (July) and Dublin taken.
1691	Athlone taken by William; Jacobite defeats follow at Aughrim, Galway, and Limerick; conflict ends with Treaty of Limerick (October) and Irish officers allowed to leave for France.
1695	Penal laws introduced to restrict rights of Catholics; banishment of Catholic clergy.
1704	Laws introduced constricting rights of Catholics in landholding and public office.
1728	Franchise removed from Catholics.
1791	Foundation of United Irishmen republican movement.
1796	French invasion force lands in Bantry Bay.
1798	Defeat of Rising in Wexford and death of United Irishmen leaders Wolfe Tone and Lord Edward Fitzgerald.

1800   Act of Union between England and
                  Ireland.
1803   Dublin Rising under Robert Emmet.
1829   Catholics allowed to sit in Parliament.
1845-1849   The Great Hunger: thousands starve to
                  death as potato crop fails and thousands
                  more emigrate.
1856   Phoenix Society founded.
1858   Irish Republican Brotherhood established.
1873   Foundation of Home Rule League.
1893   Foundation of Gaelic League.
1904   Foundation of Irish Reform Association.
1913   Dublin strikes and lockout.
1916   Easter Rising in Dublin and proclamation
                  of an Irish Republic.
1917   Irish Parliament formed after Sinn Fein
                  election victory.
1919-1921   War between Irish Republican Army and
                  British Army.
1922   Irish Free State founded, while six
                  northern counties remain part of United
                  Kingdom as Northern Ireland, or Ulster;
                  civil war up until 1923 between rival
                  republican groups.
1949   Foundation of Irish Republic after all
                  remaining constitutional links with Britain
                  are severed.